Wedding Ceremony Idea Book

GEORGE W. KNIGHT

**Sample Vows, Prayers, Scripture Readings, and
Responses To Make Your Wedding
Unique and Memorable**

Revised Edition

ISBN: 0-939298-01-5 (U.S.A.)

Printed in the United States of America

ISBN: 0-939298-01-5

CONTENTS

INTRODUCTION
A Wedding Ceremony Just for You

If you want something new and different in your wedding ceremony, this book is just what you need. It's filled with scores of suggested vows, prayers, Scripture readings, poems, and congregational responses to help you and your fiancé create a unique service of your very own. Read it over together thoroughly, then use the planning steps in Chapter 5 to complete your own ceremony. A section is provided at the end of the book for writing down every detail of your final wedding service.

Most of these ideas came from other couples just like you who wanted something a little different in their ceremony. My thanks to them for their permission to use these ideas in this resource. Their creativity proves that a wedding can be unique, personal, and contemporary — but thoroughly Christian at the same time.

George W. Knight

1
Write Your Own Ceremony: A National Trend

So you want something a little different in your wedding ceremony? Welcome to the group! During the past few years more and more engaged couples have been searching for the same thing. The typical church wedding of today is likely to include such innovations as vows that were written by the bride and groom, prayers by members of the wedding party, a welcome to the wedding guests from the bride, hymn singing and congregational responses by the wedding guests.

What's behind this trend toward variety and uniqueness in wedding ceremonies? For generations couples seemed to be content with the orderly formality of the old Protestant Episcopal service. Its Elizabethan phrases — "to have and to hold" and "thereto I pledge thee my troth" — may have seemed a little strange to modern ears. But few couples took the time to question their meaning or to update them for the twentieth century. Why the trend away from this traditional ceremony in the last few years?

If you'll think about why you want a different ceremony for your own wedding, maybe you can understand why this trend has developed.

First of all, like many couples getting married today, you're probably turned off by the formal and ritualistic approach. The informal and personal flavor means more to you. You want your wedding to be a reflection of the unique personalities of you and your fiancé. This means such personal touches as your own vows, in your own words, spoken to each other in your own unique way. Or, it may mean one of your favorite popular songs or hymns, woven into your wedding at just the right moment.

The personal can be pushed so far, of course, that it degenerates into a tasteless invasion of privacy. But if those little personal touches are handled with restraint, they can make your ceremony special to you as well as to your guests.

Another reason why many couples today are writing their own ceremonies is to put their wedding in tune with the times. They prefer a wedding with an up-to-date, contemporary sound.

It's O.K. to strive for a ceremony that's upbeat and contemporary. But your purpose should be to describe the biblical ideals about marriage in modern, understandable language — not to compromise or change the basic Christian teachings on what marriage and the family are all about. Remember, too, that many of your guests will probably be more familiar with the words and phrases from a traditional marriage ceremony. Don't use concepts and terminology so modern and far-out that these people will go away without realizing they've attended a Christian wedding.

Finally, there are those couples who want their ceremony to draw their guests into more active participation in the wedding. These couples are likely to arrange wedding services that include hymn singing, congregational responses, or the repetition of the Lord's Prayer by everyone in attendance. In recent years some couples have even scheduled their wedding as part of a regular worship service of their church. This makes the wedding a time of celebration and participation by the entire company of faith.

No matter what your reasons for writing your own ceremony, you're sure to find it a helpful exercise. One immediate benefit is that it forces you and your fiancé to think together about some of the values and goals you will work toward in your marriage. While you're writing your vows and pulling all the other elements of your ceremony together, you'll be thinking long and hard about the nature of Christian marriage and the long-range commitment you are making to each other. These mutual understandings make an excellent foundation on which to build a lasting marriage.

So welcome to the growing company of engaged couples who have taken the time to arrange and create their own wedding ceremonies. Planning this special event together should give both of you a good send-off on the life-long adventure of becoming one as husband and wife.

2
Basic Ingredients
Of a Christian Wedding
Ceremony

Before you can plan a ceremony of your own, you need to know what ingredients are usually included in a Christian wedding ceremony. Here's a quick review of the features you will find in most church weddings. You might not use all of these, of course, in your own wedding. But keep an open mind on all these possibilities as you begin your planning. Some of these features will be eliminated naturally as you begin to firm up your detailed ceremony plans.

MUSIC

Appropriate music is one of the key ingredients of a memorable wedding. Background music during the parts of the ceremony when people are speaking is strictly a no-no, since this only detracts from the beauty and solemnity of the occasion. But music of the following four distinct types at special times during the wedding lends its own unique beauty to the ceremony.

Prelude. — Quiet instrumental music by the organist or pianist is appropriate during this time while guests are being seated before the service begins. A medley of well-known hymns is always appropriate in a church wedding. In some weddings vocal music may be included as part of the prelude just before the wedding party begins to enter the church.

Processional. — The tempo of the music always picks up when the wedding party enters the church. Hymn singing by the congregation during the processional seems to be gaining in popularity in many weddings.

Recessional. — Lovely instrumental music while the wedding party leaves the church at the end of the service is a standard feature of most contemporary church weddings. Joyous and exuberant hymns of praise are appropriate during the recessional.

Vocal Music. — Vocal solos or duets at one or two places during the ceremony lend a special dignity to many church weddings. One of the most popular selections is "The Lord's Prayer," often sung by a soloist as the couple kneel in prayer following their vows or the exchange of rings. Some popular songs may also be appropriate if their lyrics have an underlying Christian message.

WORDS OF WELCOME FROM THE COUPLE

Some couples are throwing formality to the winds these days by including a personal word of welcome to the wedding guests at the beginning of the ceremony. The rationale behind this contemporary feature is that the bride and groom invited these people; so they should also welcome these guests personally and thank them for attending this special event in their lives. This welcome sometimes takes the form of a more formal word of thanks from the bride and groom in their printed wedding bulletin.

OPENING WORDS OF THE MINISTER

The introductory statement of the minister usually consists of a short summary of the meaning of marriage as revealed in the Bible. Some words are generally included about the significance of the ceremony that is about to take place. In cases where the bride and groom are well known to members of the church where the wedding is being held, the minister may include some personal words about the couple and their religious history.

PRAYERS OF THE MINISTER
AND MEMBERS OF THE WEDDING PARTY

Taking each other as husband and wife is one of the most important events in a couple's life. A happening of this magnitude demands an attitude of prayer. Every Christian wedding ceremony should include at least one or two prayers for God's guidance and direction in the life of the newlyweds. Prayers of thanksgiving for this happy occasion are also in order.

Traditionally, the officiating minister has led the prayers in a wedding ceremony. But members of the wedding party are sharing in this responsibility in many contemporary weddings. Before you as the bride or groom decide to lead a prayer at your own wedding, make sure you have nerves of steel. Sometimes the very people who scoff at the idea of being nervous at their wedding turn into basket cases before the brief service is over!

What about other members of the wedding party? Father of the groom? Mother of the bride? Best man? Maid of honor? Perhaps a prayer led by one of them could add that unforgettable touch to this special day.

SCRIPTURE PASSAGES

One or two passages of Scripture on the meaning of marriage should be included in every wedding. These are usually read by the minister, but they could also be read by any member of the wedding party.

POETRY

Love poems or special readings on marriage can also be woven into a Christian marriage ceremony, if their lyrics are appropriate and tasteful. The poems of Elizabeth Barrett Browning and Robert Browning seem to be especially suitable for this purpose. Some couples include a brief poem in their vows to each other. The officiating minister could also recite a poem of the couple's choosing. Or, an appropriate reading or poem could be repeated by the best man or the maid of honor.

THE GIVING IN MARRIAGE

The part of the ceremony where the father gives the bride away is a hold-over from ancient days when the bride was considered her father's property. Today this gesture of "giving away" symbolizes the formal consent and acknowledgment of the marriage by the families involved. In a modern church wedding the minister is likely to ask, "Who *presents* this woman to be married to this man?" rather than "Who *gives* this woman to be married to this man?"

Many couples today are asking both sets of parents to be involved in this part of the ceremony. All four parents may stand with the bride and groom at the altar to make brief statements of love and encouragement, symbolizing their best wishes for this union.

CONGREGATIONAL RESPONSES

Participation in the wedding by the guests is a high priority with many couples. They want their guests to enter into the celebration of this happy hour rather than just sit and watch as passive spectators.

One good way to get your guests involved is to include a congregational response in your ceremony. These usually take the form of a litany of praise, with the minister making certain statements about the goodness of God and the congregation responding in unison with their own words of praise. If you include a feature like this in your wedding, you'll need to provide a printed worship bulletin with all these responsive elements printed in full.

EXCHANGE OF VOWS

The heart of the Christian wedding ceremony is the exchange of vows between bride and groom. More and more couples today are writing their own vows and saying them to each other rather than repeating prescribed "formula vows" under the direction of the officiating minister.

If you write your own vows, be sure they include a pledge of your faithfulness and devotion to each other for the rest of your lives. This biblical ideal for marriage should be underscored in every Christian wedding ceremony. And keep your vows brief — no more than four or five sentences in length. This is not the place for long, rambling essays on the nature of Christian marriage. Vows should also have an intimate and personal character. Remember, you are making promises to each other — not to the congregation or to the rest of the wedding party.

EXCHANGE OF RINGS

The purpose of the exchange of rings is to seal or symbolize the pledges of devotion which you and your mate have made to each other. So this part of the ceremony always comes logically right after the exchange of vows.

Just before the exchange of rings, the minister usually makes some statement about the symbolism of the rings. This statement could be made just as easily by both of you as you slip the rings on each other's fingers. The trend in the double ring ceremony nowadays seems to be toward a simple and direct ring exchange. The bride and groom may say to each other, "I give you this ring as a symbol of my devotion. Wear it to show others that you are touched by my love."

10

LIGHTING OF THE UNITY CANDLE

In recent years more and more Christian couples have been including a custom called the lighting of the unity candle in their wedding ceremonies. This always occurs near the end of the service. The bride and groom each take a lighted candle and light a larger candle to symbolize the union of their lives in marriage.

If you include this element in your ceremony, you might decide to make some statement as husband and wife about the marriage union which has just been formed. Or, the minister might read some appropriate Scripture, such as Genesis 2:23-24, about "two becoming one," as you and your mate light the unity candle.

DECLARATION OF MARRIAGE
BY THE MINISTER

This is a formal statement by the minister that the bride and groom are now united as husband and wife. This declaration is often combined with a charge to the couple to work together to build a Christian home. Other brief comments from the minister about the holiness and permanence of marriage are also appropriate.

These, then, are the basic ingredients that you will find in most contemporary church weddings. Now take a close look at Chapter 3 to see how other couples have applied their creativity to these elements to make them unique and expressive of their Christian values.

NOTES

_____

_____

_____

_____

_____

_____

_____

_____

_____

_____

_____

_____

_____

_____

_____

_____

_____

_____

3
Sample Ingredients From Other Ceremonies

Now that you have reviewed some of the typical features of a Christian wedding ceremony (see Chapter 2), you need to take a look at what some other couples have done to put their own unique personality into these elements. The following sample ingredients have been gleaned from dozens of different ceremonies written by other couples. Read them over carefully with your fiancé. Underline or put a check mark beside those elements that appeal to you, then discuss these ideas together. This exercise should put you in touch with each other about the unique elements which you would like to include in your own ceremony.

MUSIC FOR THE WEDDING

Prelude (while the guests are being seated)

"Sweet, Sweet Spirit"
"The Wedding Song"
"Jesu, Joy of Man's Desiring"
"Blest Be the Tie That Binds"
"O Love That Wilt Not Let Me Go"
"Savior, Like a Shepherd Lead Us"
"Sheep and Lambs May Safely Graze"
"Invocation"
"Larghetto"
"Awake, My Heart, with Gladness"
"Ode to Joy"
"Love's Greeting"

13

"Praise to the Lord the Almighty"
"Arioso"
"Sarabande"
"Pastorale"
"Abide, O Dearest Jesus"

Processional (while the wedding party enters the church)

"Bridal Chorus" ("Here Comes the Bride")
"Praise the Lord! Ye Heavens Adore Him"
"Processional on Westminster Abbey"
"Joyful, Joyful, We Adore Thee"
"Trumpet Tunes"
"Processional in G Major"
"Festival March"
"Praise Ye the Father"
"To God Be the Glory"
"Fanfare"
"My Heart Ever Faithful"
"Bell Symphony"
"Praise My Soul, the King of Heaven"

Vocal music (during the ceremony)

"Sunrise, Sunset" (from *Fiddler on the Roof*)
"My Heart Ever Faithful"
"The Wedding Song"
"O Perfect Love"
"Wedding Prayer"
"Because"
"Wonderful Love"
"I Love You Truly"
"A Christian Wedding Song"
"Oh Promise Me"
"Whither Thou Goest"
"Biblical Songs"
"We've Only Just Begun"
"If We Only Have Love"
"O Lord Most Holy"
"The Greatest of These Is Love"
"Wedding Hymn"
"Our Wedding Prayer"
"The Lord's Prayer"
"Entreat Me Not to Leave Thee"

14

"Both Sides Now"
"Here at Thine Altar, Lord"
"Though I Speak with the Tongues"
"Thou Wilt Keep Him in Perfect Peace"
"Be Thou with Them"
"The King of Love My Shepherd Is"
"Whither Thou Goest"
"O Lord Most Holy"
"Set Me as a Seal Upon Thine Heart"
"O Love That Casts Out Fear"
"Psalm 150"
"If with All Your Hearts"
"The Call"
"We Lift Our Hearts to Thee"
"We've Only Just Begun"
"Turn, Turn"

Organ music (during the ceremony)

"Trumpet Voluntary"
"God's Time Is Best"
"A Joyous March"
"Suite in D Major"
"Alleluia"
"O Jesus, I Have Promised"
"O Love That Will Not Let Me Go"
"Blest Be the Tie That Binds"

Congregational hymns (during the ceremony)

"Sweet, Sweet Spirit"
"Joyful, Joyful We Adore Thee"
"Love Divine, All Loves Excelling"
"Jesus, Thou Joy of Loving Hearts"
"O Perfect Love"
"For the Beauty of the Earth"
"Saviour, Like a Shepherd Lead Us"
"All Creatures of Our God and King"
"Be Thou My Vision"
"Pass It On"
"Children of the Heavenly Father"
"Day by Day"

"Praise Ye the Lord, the Almighty"
"Like a River Glorious"
"Happy the Home"
"Fairest Lord Jesus"
"We Come, O Christ, to Thee"
"Now Thank We All Our God"
"God of Our Life, Through All the Circling Years"

Recessional (while the wedding party leaves the church)

"Wedding March"
"Trumpet Tunes"
"Hymn to Joy"
"Toccata from Symphony V"
"Now Thank We All Our God"
"All Creatures of Our God and King"
"Fanfare"
"O God, Our Help in Ages Past"
"Praise, My Soul, the King of Heaven"

WORDS OF WELCOME FROM THE COUPLE

A Home to Honor God

We are honored to have you here today as our guests. We are delighted that you can share these happy and sacred moments with us as we pledge our lives to each other in the adventure of Christian marriage. We ask your prayers and your continuing friendship as we take this step in establishing a home that will bring honor and glory to God.

Gratitude for God's Gifts

Thank you for honoring us with your presence today. Thank you for the friendship and support you have given us in the past. We hope our wedding today will be a moment when all our thoughts are turned toward God in gratitude for his gifts of love and joy.

Our Inspiration

Susan and I are delighted that you can share in our wedding today. You have helped us and encouraged us across the years in more ways than you can imagine. Thank you for giving the greatest gift anyone can give — yourselves. Your example of self-giving is our inspiration as we pledge our lives to each other in marriage today.

16

Your Part in the Gospel

Welcome to this special moment in our lives. Since Joel and I have grown up in this church, what could be more appropriate than to say our marriage vows here among all our friends, many of whom have known us since we were children. Thank you for the contribution you have made to our lives. You helped us find Christ as Savior years ago, and you have helped us grow and develop as Christians through all these years. Now we feel your support very deeply as we stand together at this important moment in our lives. Our word of thanks to you today is the prayer that the apostle Paul prayed when he thought of his Philippian friends: "I thank my God whenever I think of you; and when I pray for you all, my prayers are always joyful, because of the part you have taken in the work of the Gospel from the first day until now" (Philippians 1:3-5, NEB).

OPENING WORDS OF THE MINISTER

Woman from Man's Side

When God created man and placed him in the Garden of Eden, he realized immediately that it wasn't good for human beings to live alone. So he created a helper and companion for man. We notice from the Scriptures that God didn't take woman from man's head, lest she should rule over him, nor from his feet, lest he should trample upon her. No, he took woman from man's side, that she should be his equal, and from close to his heart, that he should love and cherish her.

The Scriptures also tell us that marriage was honored by the presence of Christ at the marriage feast in Cana of Galilee. Jesus also used the figure of marriage to symbolize that great day when he, the bridegroom, adorned in all his glory, will come for the church which he has purchased with his own blood. Marriage was also commended by the apostle Paul as a holy and honorable way of life. A marriage sanctioned by God is a union of two lives — two hearts that beat as one — so welded together that they walk and work in harmony through all the days of their lives. A husband and wife should bear each other's burdens as well as share each other's joys. This is the type of marriage that Richard and Becky seek today as they come before us to ask God's blessing upon their union.

Marriage Is Built on Love

Dear friends, we are assembled here today in the presence of God to unite Janice and Roy in marriage. The Bible teaches that marriage should be a permanent relationship of one man and one woman freely and totally committed to each other as husband and wife for a lifetime. Jesus himself declared that man shall leave his father and mother and be united with his wife in an attitude of total commitment, and the two shall become one flesh.

If marriage is to last for a lifetime, it must be built upon love. In the 13th chapter of 1 Corinthians, the apostle Paul gives a beautiful description of the type of love it takes to build a happy home: "Love is patient; love is kind and envies no one. Love is never boastful, nor conceited, nor rude; never selfish, not quick to take offense. Love keeps no score of wrongs; does not gloat over other men's sins, but delights in the truth. There is nothing love cannot face; there is no limit to its faith, its hope, and its endurance" (1 Corinthians 13:4-7, NEB).

Love like this can bring honor to God in our homes. Janice and Roy, my fervent prayer is that your marriage will always be blessed with an abundance of this kind of love.

Give Thanks to the Lord

In the early days of creation, God looked at Adam alone in the garden and declared, "It is not good that man should be alone." So he created woman to be his companion, and the first marriage relationship was established. God took the initiative in the formation of marriage because he realized our need as human beings for a deep and supportive relationship. Since that first union in the Garden of Eden, countless other couples have sought love, acceptance, and companionship in the relationship of marriage.

We have gathered here today to celebrate the union of Larry and Tricia in Christian marriage. In one sense, this is a very private moment that belongs only to them. But this event is also a public service of thanksgiving and celebration that should speak clearly to each of us. During these moments together, breathe a prayer of thanksgiving to God for his blessings in your own life. Renew your own marriage vows and pledge again your devotion to your family and friends. Ask God to use your life in his service.

Let this be a time when all of us declare with the psalmist: "I will give thanks to the Lord with my whole heart; I will tell of all thy wonderful deeds."

Marriage as God's Gift

God in his love and goodness has given marriage as a precious gift. Through this gift we can know the deepest and most fulfilling of all human relationships—one which almost touches heaven itself. It is also through this deep and abiding love of a husband and wife for each other that God brings new life into the world. Because marriage is such a sacred and holy relationship, it requires more of two people than they can offer in their own strength. But God promises to be with us in marriage to help us measure up to its responsibilities. Let us pause to thank God for the gift of marriage and his abiding presence in the union of husband and wife.

PRAYERS OF THE MINISTER
AND MEMBERS OF THE WEDDING PARTY

Thanksgiving for Love (Minister)

Our Father, thank you for the love of devoted fathers and mothers, so strong and secure that it releases the center of their affections — even their own children — that they might take this important step in marriage. Grant such unselfish love to this young couple who stand before you now in this act of commitment to each other as husband and wife. May their love for each other grow stronger with the passing years. Give them love and grace enough to forgive each other during those turbulent times in their relationship. Grant them also the gift of celebration so they can enjoy the many happy times they will share together as husband and wife. Most of all, Lord, keep their attention focused on you, the author and perfector of every good gift of love. Through Jesus Christ our Lord. Amen.

Prayer for Happiness (Minister)

Almighty God our Father, who makes all of life worth living, thank you for this present moment of joy when your grace is revealed in a special way. Thank you for this young couple, Faye and Fred, who are pledging their devotion to each other and to you through this marriage ceremony. Thank you for the combination of circumstances and events which brought them together and nurtured their love for each other. Thank you for the Christian influences of the homes in which they grew up. Thank you for the support and encouragement of their friends who share in their happiness during this memorable moment in their lives.

Most of all, Lord, thank you for your affirmation and blessing of marriage as life's most sacred human relationship. Grant that Faye and Fred in their life together will find the supreme happiness and joy which you desire for all your children. In Jesus' name. Amen.

19

Prayer on Our Wedding Day (Bride or Groom)

Lord, our hearts are overflowing with happiness on this our wedding day. Thank you for bringing us together and for directing us every step of the way as we made our marriage plans. Thank you also for these our friends who have come to celebrate these moments with us. Grant that everything that is done here today will bring honor and glory to your name. Bless our marriage and the home that we are establishing together. Help us to continue to grow in our love for each other. Make us thoughtful and understanding helpmates and companions. And guide us and walk beside us during all our days together as husband and wife. In Jesus' name. Amen.

Prayer for the Couple (Groom's Father or Best Man)

Lord, thank you for the greatest gift in the world — the gift of love. Thank you for this occasion that reminds us once again of what a precious thing love is. Thank you for the love that Bob and Dorothy pledge to each other today as they begin the thrilling adventure of building a life together. We thank you also, Lord, for the privilege of being here today and participating in this beautiful ceremony. Let it serve as a reminder to us of the deep meaning of marriage — that two people can become more than they are individually because of their relationship. Help Bob and Dorothy to capitalize on the strength of their relationship, to lean on each other, and to build up one another during all their future days together. Grant that their love, as beautiful as it is in this hour, will grow even deeper and stronger in the years ahead. In Jesus' name. Amen.

Responsive Prayer by Congregation

(The following prayer could be prayed responsively by the minister and the wedding guests at the conclusion of the ceremony. The prayer could be included in the printed wedding bulletin for use by the guests.

MINISTER: Father, look with favor upon this man and this woman whom you have made one in holy matrimony.

CONGREGATION: Give them wisdom and devotion in the ordering of their common life, that each may be to the other a strength in need, a counselor in

	perplexity, a comfort in sorrow, and a companion in joy.
MINISTER:	Grant that their wills may be so knit together in your will, and their spirits in your spirit, that they may grow in love and peace with you and each other all the days of their life.
CONGREGATION:	Give them grace, when they hurt each other, to recognize and acknowledge their fault and to seek each other's forgiveness as well as yours.
MINISTER:	Make their life together a sign of Christ's love to this sinful and broken world, that unity may overcome estrangement, forgiveness may heal guilt, and joy may conquer despair.
CONGREGATION:	Give them such fulfillment of their mutual affection that they may reach out in love and concern for others.
MINISTER:	Grant that all married persons who have witnessed these vows may find their lives strengthened and their loyalties confirmed.
UNISON:	Grant that your will may be done on earth as it is in heaven, where you, O Father, with your Son and the Holy Spirit live and reign together, both now and forever more. Amen.

SCRIPTURE PASSAGES

Man and Woman Made for Each Other

Then the Lord God said, "It is not good for the man to live alone. I will make a suitable companion to help him." So he took some soil from the ground and formed all the animals and all the birds. Then he brought them to the man to see what he would name them; and that is how they all got their names. So the man named all the birds and all the animals; but not one of them was a suitable companion to help him.

Then the Lord God made the man fall into a deep sleep, and while he was sleeping, he took out one of the man's ribs and closed up the flesh. He formed a woman out of the rib and brought her to him. Then the man said, "At last, here is one of my own kind — Bone taken from my bone, and flesh from my flesh. 'Woman' is her name because she was taken out of man." That is why a man leaves his father and mother and is united with his wife, and they become one. — Genesis 2:18-24, TEV.

The Nature of True Love

I may be able to speak the languages of men and even of angels, but if I have no love, my speech is no more than a noisy gong or a clanging bell. I may have the gift of inspired preaching; I may have all knowledge and understand all secrets; I may have all the faith needed to move mountains — but if I have no love, I am nothing. I may give away everything I have, and even give up my body to be burned — but if I have no love, this does me no good.

Love is patient and kind; it is not jealous or conceited or proud; love is not ill-mannered or selfish or irritable; love does not keep a record of wrongs; love is not happy with evil, but is happy with the truth. Love never gives up; and its faith, hope, and patience never fail. — 1 Corinthians 13:1-7, TEV.

Forgiveness Essential in Marriage

You are the people of God; he loved you and chose you for his own. So then, you must clothe yourselves with compassion, kindness, humility, gentleness, and patience. Be tolerant with one another and forgive one another whenever any of you has a complaint against someone else. You must forgive one another just as the Lord has forgiven you. And to all these qualities add love, which binds all things together in perfect unity. — Colossians 3:12-14, TEV.

Ruth's Pledge of Faithfulness

And Ruth said, Entreat me not to leave thee, or to return from following after thee: for whither thou goest, I will go; and where thou lodgest, I will lodge: thy people shall be my people, and thy God my God: Where thou diest, will I die, and there will I be buried: the Lord do so to me, and more also, if ought but death part thee and me. — Ruth 1:16-17, KJV.

Enter His Gates with Thanksgiving

Make a joyful noise unto the Lord, all ye lands. Serve the Lord with gladness: come before his presence with singing. Know ye that the Lord he is God: it is he that hath made us, and not we ourselves; we are his people, and the sheep of his pasture.

Enter into his gates with thanksgiving, and into his courts with praise: be thankful unto him, and bless his name. For the Lord is good; his mercy is everlasting; and his truth endureth to all generations. — Psalm 100, KJV.

Blessings of a Godly Home

Blessed is every one who fears the Lord, who walks in his ways! You shall eat the fruit of the labor of your hands; you shall be happy, and it shall be well with you.

Your wife will be like a fruitful vine within your house; your children will be like olive shoots around your table. Lo, thus shall the man be blessed who fears the Lord. — Psalm 128:1-4, RSV.

Duties of Husbands and Wives to Each Other

Submit yourselves to one another because of your reverence for Christ. Wives, submit yourselves to your husbands as to the Lord. For a husband has authority over his wife just as Christ has authority over the church; and Christ is himself the Savior of the church, his body. And so wives must submit themselves completely to their husbands just as the church submits itself to Christ.

Husbands, love your wives just as Christ loved the church and gave his life for it. He did this to dedicate the church to God by his word, after making it clean by washing it in water, in order to present the church to himself in all its beauty — pure and faultless, without spot or wrinkle or any other imperfection. Men ought to love their wives just as they love their own bodies. A man who loves his wife loves himself. (No one ever hates his own body. Instead, he feeds it and takes care of it, just as Christ does the church; for we are members of his body.) As the scripture says, "For this reason a man will leave his father and mother and unite with his wife, and the two will become one."

There is a deep secret truth revealed in this scripture, which I understand as applying to Christ and the church. But it also applies to you: every husband must love his wife as himself, and every wife must respect her husband. — Ephesians 5:21-33, TEV.

We Love Because God First Loved Us

Dear friends, let us love one another, because love comes from God. Whoever loves is a child of God and knows God. Whoever does not love does not know God, for God is love. And God showed his love for us by sending his only Son into the world, so that we might have life through him. This is what love is: it is not that we have loved God, but that he loved us and sent his Son to be the means by which our sins are forgiven.

Dear friends, if this is how God loved us, then we should love one another. No one has ever seen God, but if we love one another, God lives in union with us, and his love is made perfect in us. — 1 John 4:7-12, TEV.

Jesus' Commandment: Love One Another

 My commandment is this: love one another, just as I love you. The greatest love a person can have for his friends is to give his life for them. And you are my friends if you do what I command you. I do not call you servants any longer, because a servant does not know what his master is doing. Instead, I call you friends, because I have told you everything I heard from my Father. You did not choose me; I chose you and appointed you to go and bear much fruit, the kind of fruit that endures. And so the Father will give you whatever you ask of him in my name. This, then, is what I command you: love one another. — John 15:12-17, TEV.

A Miracle at a Wedding

Two days later there was a wedding in the town of Cana in Galilee. Jesus' mother was there, and Jesus and his disciples had also been invited to the wedding. When the wine had given out, Jesus' mother said to him, "They are out of wine."

"You must not tell me what to do," Jesus replied. "My time has not yet come."

Jesus' mother then told the servants, "Do whatever he tells you."

The Jews have rules about ritual washing, and for this purpose six stone water jars were there, each one large enough to hold between twenty and thirty gallons. Jesus said to the servants, "Fill these jars with water." They filled them to the brim, and then he told them, "Now draw some water out and take it to the man in charge of the feast." They took him the water, which now had turned into wine, and he tasted it. He did not know where this wine had come from (but, of course, the servants who had drawn out the water knew); so he called the bridgroom and said to him, "Everyone else serves the best wine first, and after the guests have drunk a lot, he serves the ordinary wine. But you have kept the best wine until now!"

Jesus performed his first miracle in Cana in Galilee; there he revealed his glory, and his disciples believed in him. — John 2:1-11, TEV.

A Time for Everything

To everything there is a season, and a time to every purpose under the heaven:

A time to be born, and a time to die; a time to plant, and a time to pluck up that which is planted.

A time to kill, and a time to heal; a time to break down, and a time to build up.

A time to weep, and a time to laugh; a time to mourn, and a time to dance.

A time to cast away stones, and a time to gather stones together; a time to embrace, and a time to refrain from embracing.

A time to get, and a time to lose; a time to keep, and a time to cast away.

A time to rend, and a time to sew; a time to keep silence, and a time to speak.

A time to love, and a time to hate; a time of war, and a time of peace.

To everything there is a season, and a time to every purpose under the heaven. — Ecclesiastes 3:1-8, KJV.

Our Assurance of God's Eternal Love

Who, then, can separate us from the love of Christ? Can trouble do it, or hardship or persecution or hunger or poverty or danger or death? As the scripture says, "For your sake we are in danger of death at all times; we are treated like sheep that are going to be slaughtered."

No, in all these things we have complete victory through him who loved us! For I am certain that nothing can separate us from his love, neither death nor life, neither angels nor other heavenly rulers or powers, neither the present nor the future, neither the world above nor the world below — there is nothing in all creation that will ever be able to separate us from the love of God which is ours through Christ Jesus our Lord. — Romans 8:35-39, TEV.

POETRY

How Do I Love Thee?

How do I love thee! Let me count the ways.
I love thee to the depth and breadth and height
My soul can reach, when feeling out of sight
For the ends of Being and ideal Grace.
I love thee to the level of everyday's

Most quiet need, by sun and candle-light.
I love thee freely, as men strive for Right;
I love thee purely, as they turn from Praise.
I love thee with the passion put to use
In my old griefs, and with my childhood's faith.
I love thee with a love I seemed to lose
With my lost saints, — I love thee with the breath,
Smiles, tears, of all my life! — and, If God choose,
I shall but love thee better after death.
— Elizabeth Barrett Browning

 ## Our Lord Directs Our Way

God does not lead us year by year
    Nor even day by day,
But step by step our path unfolds,
    Our Lord directs our way.

Tomorrow's plans we do not know,
    We only know this minute!
But He will say, "This is the way,
    By faith now walk ye in it."

And we are glad that it is so;
    Today is ours to share,
And when tomorrow comes, His grace
    Shall far exceed its care.

What need to worry then or fret?
    The God who gave His only Son
Holds all our moments in His hand
    And gives them one by one.
— author unknown

The Night Has A Thousand Eyes

The night has a thousand eyes,
    And the day but one;
Yet the light of the bright world dies
    With the dying sun.

The mind has a thousand eyes,
    And the heart but one;
Yet the light of a whole life dies
    When love is done.
— Francis William Bourdillon

If Thou Must Love Me

If thou must love me, let it be for naught
Except for love's sake only. Do not say
"I love her for her smile — her look — her way
Of speaking gently, — for a trick of thought
That falls in well with mine, and certes brought
A sense of pleasant ease on such a day" —
For these things in themselves, Beloved, may
Be changed, or change for thee — and love, so wrought,
May be unwrought so. Neither love me for
Thine own dear pity's wiping my cheeks dry:
A creature might forget to weep, who bore
Thy comfort long, and love thy love thereby!
But love me for love's sake, that evermore
Thou mayst love on, through love's eternity.
                    — Elizabeth Barrett Browning

I Wish You Love

I do not wish you joy without a sorrow,
    Nor endless day without the healing dark,
Nor brilliant sun without the restful shadow,
    Nor tides that never turn against your bark.

I wish you love, and strength, and wisdom,
    And gold enough to help some needy one,
I wish you songs, but also blessed silence,
    And God's sweet peace when every day is done.
                    — author unknown

The Nature of True Love

Let me not to the marriage of true minds
Admit impediments. For love is not love
Which alters when it alteration finds
Or bends with the remover to remove.
O, no! it is an ever-fixed mark
That looks on tempests and is never shaken;
It is the star to every wand'ring bark,
Whose worth's unknown although his height be taken.
Love's not Time's fool, though rosy lips and cheeks
Within his bending sickle's compass come.
Love alters not with his brief hours and weeks,

27

But bears it out even to the edge of doom.
  If this be error, and upon me proved,
  I never writ, nor no man ever loved.
        — From *A Midsummer Night's Dream*
        by William Shakespeare

THE GIVING IN MARRIAGE

Will You Support This Couple?

(The following remarks are directed by the minister to the bride's parents and the groom's parents as they stand at the altar with their son and daughter at the beginning of the ceremony.)

This occasion is a special kind of celebration for your parents who have brought these children into the world and nurtured them to adulthood. Today you are witnessing another stage in the lives of your son and daughter. Your continuing support and encouragement as Christian parents will be needed as Becky and Allan unite in marriage and set about the task of building a home of their own. Mr. and Mrs. Green and Mr. and Mrs. Ramsey, are you willing to undergird and support this marriage with your love and concern?

(The parents should respond in unison, "We are.")

Accept Our Daughter As Your Own

(The following remarks are directed by the father of the bride to the groom's parents and then to the groom at the beginning of the ceremony.)

To the groom's parents: Mr. and Mrs. Jenkins, my wife and I are pleased to ask you to accept our daughter, Karen, as your daughter, too. Thank you for the Christian values which you have taught your son. We have grown to love and respect Richard, and we are pleased today to receive him into our hearts as a son.

To the groom: Richard, we are pleased to present our daughter, Karen, to be joined to you as wife during this ceremony. We have come to know you as a person of Christian integrity who is seeking to follow God's will. We proudly receive you today as a son. We commit Karen to you in complete confidence that you will care for her needs and seek to make her happy in Christian love and marriage.

Including Parents in the Vows

(The following unique vows from a ceremony show how both sets of parents can be included in a show of support for their children on this significant occasion in their lives. This is a good alternative to the traditional "giving away" of the bride by her father.)

MINISTER:	Robert, Karen has indicated she wants to be your wife. Will you give yourself to her? Will you try to share completely with her in your life together? Will you promise to be open and honest in your relationship? Will you give her all comfort and support and strength?
GROOM:	I will.
MINISTER:	Karen, Robert has indicated he wants to be your husband. Will you give yourself to him? Will you try to share completely with him in your life together? Will you try always to be open and honest in your relationship? Will you promise to give him all comfort and support and strength?
BRIDE:	I will.
MINISTER:	In marriage, two people leave established families and begin a new life together. Mr. and Mrs. Johnson and Mr. and Mrs. Shapiro, will you try, with the greatest love and wisdom you can command, to support this new couple and to help them in every way?
PARENTS:	We will.
MINISTER:	Karen and Robert, you may now pledge your vows to each other.
GROOM:	I, Robert, take you, Karen, to be my wife; and I promise in the midst of our families and friends and in the presence of God to stand beside and with you always; in times of celebration and times of sadness; in times of pleasure and times of anger; in times of pain and times of health; I will live with you and love you as long as we both shall live.

29

BRIDE:	I, Karen, take you, Robert, to be my husband; and I promise in the midst of our families and friends and in the presence of God to stand beside and with you always; in times of celebration and times of sadness; in times of pleasure and times of anger; in times of pain and times of health; I will live with you and love you as long as we both shall live.

CONGREGATIONAL RESPONSES

We Give You Thanks, O Lord

MINISTER:	Great is the Lord and greatly to be praised! He is gracious and merciful, slow to anger, and abounding in steadfast love.
CONGREGATION:	We give you thanks, O Lord.
MINISTER:	The Lord is just in all his ways and kind in all his doings.
CONGREGATION:	We give you thanks, O Lord.
MINISTER:	The Lord is near to all who call upon him. He gives graciously to all. For the gift of human life: for the variety of our skills; for our different ways of thinking and moving and speaking; for our common hardships and common hopes we have from birth till death.
CONGREGATION:	We give you thanks, O Lord.
MINISTER:	For his blessing upon the institution of marriage; for the mystery and joy of flesh made one; for mutual forgiveness and burdens shared; for secrets kept in love.
CONGREGATION:	We give you thanks, O Lord.
MINISTER:	For children and the hope for tomorrow which they represent; for their fresh ideas and unending energy.
CONGREGATION:	We give you thanks, O Lord.
MINISTER:	For the process of growing up and growing

old; for wisdom mellowed by experience; for counsel and advice and teaching.

CONGREGATION: We give you thanks, O Lord.

MINISTER: For fellowship and the opportunity to share openly and freely with those in our midst.

CONGREGATION: We give you thanks, O Lord.

MINISTER: And for Jesus Christ our Lord, who lived that we may know the love of God, who taught us the meaning of responsibility in our relationships with others, who died in obedience to that which is morally right, and who lives again to give us hope for the future.

CONGREGATION: We give you thanks, O Lord.

Love One Another

MINISTER: Dear friends, let us practice loving one another, for love comes from God and those who are loving and kind show that they are the children of God, and that they are getting to know him better.

CONGREGATION: God showed us how much he loved us by sending his only Son into the world to bring to us eternal life through his death.

MINISTER: Dear friends, since God loved us as much as that, we surely ought to love one another, too.

CONGREGATION: For though we have never seen God with our eyes, when we love each other God lives in us and his love within us grows stronger day by day.

MINISTER: We know how much God loves us because we have felt his love and because we believe him when he tells us that he loves us dearly. God is love, and anyone who lives in love is living with God and God is living in him.

CONGREGATION: And as we live with Christ, our love grows
                 more perfect and complete; so we will not be
                 ashamed and embarrassed at the day of judg-
                 ment. We can face him with confidence and
                 joy, because he loves us and we love him, too.

MINISTER: God made man like his Maker. Like God did
                 God make man; man and woman did he make
                 them.

CONGREGATION: The man who finds a wife finds a good thing.
                 She is a blessing to him from the Lord.

MINISTER: Man is joined to his wife in such a way that the
                 two become one flesh.

God Saw That It Was Good

MINISTER: In the beginning God created the heavens and
                 the earth.

CONGREGATION: And God said, let us make man in our image,
                 after our likeness;

MINISTER: And let them have dominion over the fish of
                 the sea and over the fowl of the air, and over
                 the cattle.

CONGREGATION: And over all the earth and over every creep-
                 ing thing that creepeth upon the earth.

MINISTER: So God created man in his own image; in the
                 image of God created he them.

CONGREGATION: And God blessed them, and God said unto
                 them, Be fruitful, and multiply and replenish
                 the earth.

UNISON: And God saw everything that he had made
                 and behold, it was very good, and the evening
                 and the morning were the sixth day.

We Promise to Support Them

MINISTER: Richard and Julie ask for our prayers and support as they begin the adventure of marriage together.

CONGREGATION: We promise to uphold them in our thoughts and prayers as they work at building a deep and abiding love.

MINISTER: Those of us who have been married for several years realize that genuine love is not easily achieved. Richard and Julie will need determination and patience to renew their vows year after year—to cultivate their love for each other.

CONGREGATION: We promise to support them in every appropriate way as they work at this task in their marriage.

MINISTER: We also realize that genuine love is fulfilled only as it reaches out to others. We ask that the special kind of love which Richard and Julie feel for each other might reach out beyond themselves to their family, their friends, and the larger world in which they live.

CONGREGATION: We promise to return this love as it flows out to us. And we, in turn, will pass this love on to the larger universe in which we dwell. This is God's purpose in giving us the gift of love—that it might grow and multiply to bless the lives of others.

EXCHANGE OF VOWS

To Respect Your Individuality

(Directed by the bride to the groom as they hold hands and face each other.)

I love you, Harold, and I want to be your wife and helpmate. In marriage I promise to consider your interests and not merely my own. With divine assistance, I promise to show you love, joy, peace, patience, kindness, goodness, faithfulness, gentleness, and self-control. I promise to communicate with you as openly and honestly as I can and will share with you my life, feelings, hopes, joys, frustrations, disappointments, anxieties, and dreams and will listen as you share with me. I will try to meet your needs and will respect your individuality as well as my own. I will work with you to build a lasting relationship of love and commitment for the glory and honor of God. I give myself freely to you, Harold, for as long as we both shall live.

To Love You as I Love Myself

(Directed to the bride by the groom as they hold hands and face each other.)

I love you, Donna, and I want to be your husband and companion. I promise to try to love you as I love myself. Under the guidance of our Lord and Savior Jesus Christ, I promise to show love, joy, peace, patience, kindness, goodness, faithfulness, gentleness, and self-control. I promise to communicate with you as honestly and openly as I can; to share my life — my hopes, dreams, disappointments, frustrations — and to share my feelings and to listen to you as you share with me. I will try to meet your needs and to respect your individuality. I will work with you to build and establish a lasting relationship of love and commitment for the glory and honor of God. I give myself freely to you, Donna, for as long as we both shall live.

In Sickness and in Health

(Directed by the minister to the couple as they hold hands and face each other.)

Edward, will you take Brenda to be your wife? Will you commit yourself to her happiness and her self-fulfillment as a person, and to her usefulness in God's kingdom? Will you promise to love, honor, trust, and serve her in sickness and in health, in adversity and prosperity, and to be true and loyal to her, so long as you both shall live? (The groom should respond, "I will.")

Brenda, will you take Edward to be your husband? Will you commit yourself to his happiness and his self-fulfillment as a person, and to his usefulness in God's kingdom? Will you promise to love, honor, trust, and serve him in sickness and in health, in adversity and prosperity, and to be true and loyal to him, so long as you both shall live? (The bride should respond, "I will.")

I Choose You

(Repeated by the bride and groom individually as they hold hands and face each other.)

Wanda (Joseph), today I choose you to be my wife (husband), my friend, my love, and mother (father) of our children. I celebrate the relationship we have enjoyed since we met each other, and I look forward to the continuing development of our relationship in the days ahead. I promise to remain true to you in all the circumstances of life — in plenty and in want, in sickness and in health, in failure as well as in success. I will cherish and respect you, comfort and support you, so long as we both shall live. I willingly accept the responsibilities as well as the privileges that are involved in becoming a husband (wife).

Entreat Me Not to Leave Thee

(Repeated by the bride and groom individually as they hold hands and face each other.)

In the presence of God and this company of our family and friends, I, William (Diane), take thee, Diane (William), to be my beloved wife (husband). I promise to be faithful and true to you for the rest of my life. Entreat me not to leave thee, or to return from following after thee. For whither thou goest I will go; and where thou lodgest, I will lodge. Thy people shall be my people, and thy God my God (Ruth 1:16).

To Cherish and Honor You

(Directed by the bride to the groom as they hold hands and face each other.)

Bruce, I promise to encourage you, pray for you, and always seek to be a helper and companion in our marriage. I promise to work toward openness in our relationship, witholding nothing, and sharing willingly with you my deepest thoughts. In cultivating a spirit of genuine Christian love, I will try to be patient and kind—not jealous, boastful, or arrogant. I will not insist on my own way or be irritable or resentful. I will try to develop a love that keeps no record of your wrongs but always rejoices in the truth. Throughout our life together, I promise to cherish and honor you above all others as my beloved and my friend.

Rejoice in the Wonder of Love

(The bride and groom repeat the following vows in dialogue form as they hold hands and face each other.)

GROOM:	Sandy, I have looked forward to this day for a long time. You have made me very happy by consenting to become my wife.
BRIDE:	It is a joyful day—a time for celebration. It's good to celebrate the goodness of God's love and the joy of human love here in the company of our friends.
GROOM:	On this special day, Sandy, I pledge to love you forever. I will cherish and honor you above all others so long as we both shall live.
BRIDE:	I also pledge my love to you, Byron. I will honor and cherish you above all others so long as we both shall live.
GROOM:	I will share my life with you.
BRIDE:	And I will share my life with you.
GROOM:	I promise to help you grow as a person and to become everything you are capable of becoming.
BRIDE:	And I will support and encourage you through all the circumstances of life.
UNISON:	This is the first of many days together. Let us rejoice in the wonder of love.

What Promises Do You Make?

(These vows require a brief introduction by the minister as well as interaction with him by the bride and groom as they pledge their vows to each other in their own words.)

MINISTER:	The heart of any marriage are the promises and commitments which the husband and wife make to each other. Roger and Joyce stand before us today to declare their promises openly and gladly. Roger, what promises do you make to Joyce?
GROOM:	I promise to love you, Joyce, for the rest of our lives with all my heart and mind and strength. I promise to be faithful to you in thought, word, and deed. I gladly accept the responsibilities as well as the joys of becoming your husband.
MINISTER:	Joyce, what promises do you make to Roger?
BRIDE:	I promise to love you, Roger, for the rest of our lives with all my heart and soul and strength. I promise to

	be faithful to you in thought, word, and deed. And I gladly accept the responsibilities as well as the joys of becoming your wife.
MINISTER:	Do both of you, before these witnesses, promise to do everything in your power to make this a happy and lasting marriage?
UNISON:	We do.

EXCHANGE OF RINGS

Place the Ring . . . and Repeat After Me

(The following is the longer version of the traditional double ring ceremony, with most of the talking done by the minister.)

The perfect circle of a ring symbolizes eternity. Gold is the symbol of all that is pure and holy. Our prayer is that your love for each other will be as eternal and everlasting as these rings. In the years to come these rings should remind you of the overwhelming joy of this special occasion when you were united in marriage. Jeff (Pam), do you give this ring to Pam (Jeff) as a token of your love for her (him)? (The groom (bride) should respond, "I do.") Then place the ring on her (his) finger and repeat after me:

I, Jeff (Pam), take thee, Pam (Jeff),
To be my wedded wife (husband),
To have and to hold from this day forward;
For better, for worse,
For richer, for poorer,
In sickness and in health;
To love and to cherish 'til death do us part,
According to God's holy ordinance —
And with this ring I pledge thee my love.

I Give You This Ring

(Many couples are using a shorter version of the exchange of rings, making a simple statement about the significance of the rings as they place them on each other's finger. Any of the following short declarations are appropriate.)

"I give you this ring as a lasting reminder of my vows and as a symbol of my love and commitment."

"Barbara (Robert), take this ring as a sign of my love and fidelity."

37

"This ring is a symbol of my love and faithfulness."

"Take this ring and wear it as a sign of our marriage vows and of our faithful love for each other."

"I offer you this ring as a symbol of my enduring love. I ask that you wear it to show others that you are touched by my love."

"I give you this sign of our love — an everlasting symbol of the vows we have made to each other here today."

LIGHTING OF THE UNITY CANDLE

A New Relationship

(Spoken by the minister as the bride and groom each take a candle and light one central candle together.)

It is written in the Scriptures that the man shall leave his family and the woman shall leave her home and the two shall become as one in a new relationship. "So they are no longer two but one," Jesus declared. "What therefore God has joined together, let no man put asunder" (Matthew 19:6, RSV).

Separate but One

(Directed to the couple by the minister.)

Darlene and Andy, will each of you now take a candle to symbolize your individual lives. Now use these candles to light the central candle as a symbol of the new relationship you are beginning today. Let me remind you that marriage doesn't wipe out our separate identity as individuals. But it does enrich all our natural skills and abilities by helping us to grow and develop as people who are made in the image of God. If each of you will contribute your very best to your marriage, you will become as one in life's most intimate and fulfilling relationship. This is our prayer for both of you as you begin this exciting journey together.

Union and Identity

(Spoken by the minister as the couple light the unity candle but leave their own separate candles burning.)

Marriage brings two people into a unique relationship. In their union they share many experiences as if they were one person. But each member of this relationship also retains his own identity. Genuine love allows us to overcome our sense of loneliness and isolation, yet permits us our uniqueness as individuals. The beautiful paradox of Christian marriage is that two people become as one (bride and groom light the unity candle), and yet they remain as two individuals (bride and groom place their individual candles, still burning, on the altar), created in the image of God.

DECLARATION OF MARRIAGE
BY THE MINISTER

Become as One

Betty and Keith, it is now my joy to declare you husband and wife since you have willingly committed yourselves to each other for the rest of your lives. I charge you to become as one in your relationship in the days ahead. Fulfill your promises to each other. Love and serve the Lord. Let nothing separate you from each other.

Submit Yourself to One Another

Larry and Ann, we have listened prayerfully today to your mutual pledges of love and devotion. Neither you nor your family and friends will ever forget this day and the happiness which it brought to your lives. As your fellow Christians, we promise that we will continue to love and support you as you build a life together in the adventure of Christian marriage.

Learning to live together happily is a lifetime task; and I charge both of you during the days ahead to remember the apostle Paul's words in Ephesians: "Submit yourselves to one another, because of your reverence for Christ." Now, by the authority of God and in accordance with the laws of this state, I pronounce you husband and wife.

NOTES

40

4
Mixing the Ingredients Together: Six Unique and Contemporary Ceremonies

You should have picked up some good ideas about the features you would like to include in your own wedding service from the sample ingredients in Chapter 3. Now let's look at a representative sampling of several complete ceremonies to see how you can mix these ingredients together to form a ceremony that is uniquely your own.

You may decide to use one of these ceremonies almost exactly as it is printed here. Or, you could combine two or three of these services into one ceremony that seems to suit your personality as a couple a little better. You could even use one of these ceremonies as a base, replacing certain features with ingredients from Chapter 3 that you like even better.

All the following ceremonies have been arranged and composed by couples just like you. Each is unique and contemporary — but thoroughly Christian. Some of the ideas are sure to appeal to you as you search for the "just right" touch for your own wedding ceremony.

A MIXTURE
OF TRADITIONAL AND CONTEMPORARY

The following ceremony is a good example of the union of traditional and contemporary elements in a service of Christian marriage. Notice that the vows and the double ring ceremony retained many of the traditional phrases from weddings of the past, such as "in sickness and in health," "to have and to hold." But other parts of these vows were recast in simple, direct language.

The comments of the minister also blended traditional values about marriage with contemporary ideas about the nature of the marriage relationship. The lighting of the unity candle at the end of the ceremony was a contemporary practice, but even this was done with a traditional interpretation of the biblical meaning of "one flesh."

Opening Words of the Minister

We are gathered here today in the sight of God and in the presence of this company to witness the union of Barbara Ann Crawford and Edward Troy Hodges in Christian marriage. May our Heavenly Father look down upon this event with his smile of approval. May the Lord Jesus Christ be present and add his blessing. May the Holy Spirit attend and seal these vows in love. For marriage is a gift given by God to promote social order and to increase human happiness.

When God created man and placed him in the Garden of Eden, he saw immediately that it was not good for man to live alone. So he prepared a helper and a companion for man. In this act of creation, God didn't take the woman from man's head, lest she should rule over him, nor from his feet, lest he should trample upon her — but from his side, that she should be equal with him, and from close to his heart, that he should love, cherish, and honor her. Then he presented woman to man to serve as his helper and companion. Marriage is God's good gift to deliver us from our isolation and loneliness. This is why the book of Genesis declares, "Therefore shall a man leave his father and his mother, and shall cleave unto his wife: and they shall be one flesh" (Genesis 2:24).

Giving in Marriage

Minister: Who, then, presents Barbara to be married to Edward?
Father: Her mother and I do.

Prayer by the Minister

Our Father, thank you for the love of devoted fathers and mothers, so strong and secure and unthreatened that it releases the center of their affections — even their own children — that they might take this important step in marriage. Grant such unselfish love to this young couple who stand before you now in this act of commitment to each other. May their love for each other grow stronger with the passing years. Give them love and grace enough to forgive each other during those turbulent times in their relationship. Grant them also the gift of celebration so they can enjoy the many happy times they will share together as husband and wife. Most of all, Lord, keep their attention focused on you, the author and perfector of every good gift of love. Through Jesus Christ our Lord. Amen.

Further Comments by the Minister

Barbara and Edward, as you prepare to pledge your vows to each other, let me remind you that marriage made in heaven is a union of two lives — two hearts that beat as one — so welded together that they walk and work in love. A husband and wife should bear each other's burdens as well as share each other's joys. Remember that you will have to cultivate the art of living together — that you should be considerate, loving, and tenderhearted, upholding each other in love. The vows which you are about to take should be as binding in adversity as they are in prosperity. They should be broken only by death.

Exchange of Vows

Minister: As a symbol of your union, will you now join hands. Edward, in taking Barbara to be your wife, I require you to promise to love and cherish her, to honor and sustain her, in sickness as in health, in poverty as in wealth, in the bad that may darken your days, in the good that may brighten your ways, and to be true to her until death alone shall part you. Do you so promise?
Groom: I do.
Minister: Barbara, in taking Edward to be your husband, I require you to promise to love and cherish him, to honor and sustain him, in sickness as in health, in poverty as in wealth, in the bad that may darken your days, in the good that may brighten your ways, and to be true to him until death alone shall part you. Do you so promise?
Bride: I do.

Exchange of Rings

Minister: Now you will seal your vows by the giving and receiving of rings. The perfect circle of a ring symbolizes eternity. Gold is the symbol of all that is pure and holy. Our prayer is that your love and happiness together will be as unending and eternal as these rings. Edward, place this ring on Barbara's finger and repeat after me:

I, Edward, take thee, Barbara,
To be my wedded wife —
To have and to hold from this day forward;
For better, for worse,
For richer, for poorer,
In sickness and in health,
To love and to cherish 'til death do us part —
According to God's holy ordinance,
And with this ring I pledge you my love.

Minister: Barbara, place this ring on Edward's finger and repeat after me. (The bride repeats the same ring vow as the groom.)

Declaration of Marriage

Minister: Edward and Barbara, in these moments I have heard you pledge your love and faith to each other. Your friends and family members assembled here have heard you seal your solemn vows of marriage by giving and receiving the rings. Now it is my joy and personal privilege to declare you husband and wife.

Lighting of the Unity Candle

Minister (as bride and groom light the central candle with their individual candles): The Bible declares that the man shall leave his family and the woman shall leave her home and they shall become as one in a new relationship. As it was in the beginning, it is now until the end. Woman draws her life from man and gives it back again in love and devotion.

Introduction of the Newlyweds

Minister: Friends and family of the bride and groom, it is my pleasure to present to you Mr. and Mrs. Edward Troy Hodges.

DOUBLE VOWS
WITH A TOUCH OF ROSES

This unusual ceremony featured two different sets of vows for the bride and groom. The first called for a simple "I will" from the couple, while the second required them to repeat the vows after the minister. Because of the length of these vows, the couple made their ring exchange very brief and direct. This part of the service took the form of an intimate moment between them as they gave and received the rings.

Another unusual touch was the presentation of roses to their mothers and fathers at the end of the service to symbolize the contribution which their parents had made to their lives.[1]

Opening Words of the Minister

Happy is the day when a man and a woman come together to join their two lives into one. God looks with favor upon the sacred covenant made between a husband and wife. In marriage a man and a woman willingly bind themselves together in love to become one, even as Christ is one with the Church, his body.

God created us for togetherness. Richard and Debbie, you are about to launch upon an experience that is filled with pleasure, excitement, risk, and sometimes danger. From this day forward you must decide what it means to you to be husband and wife. The words you say today come easy, but nothing will be harder than trying to live them day after day in your home. What you promise today must be renewed tomorrow. At the conclusion of this ceremony you will legally be husband and wife, but both of you must work together year after year to keep your relationship alive and strong.

It is with great pleasure that those of us present can share these significant moments with you. We pledge ourselves to help you achieve the greatest happiness possible. We believe that what you are doing here today is an honor to God, to your church, and to your community. We pray that your marriage will be a pillar of strength to all who know you. May our great God bless you and keep you under his constant care.

Prayer of the Minister

Eternal Father, apart from you no promise or vow is sure. We ask for you to bless and guide Richard and Debbie on their journey into marriage. Keep them ever mindful of the promises they will make to each other today. Fill them with such love and joy that they may build a home where no one is a stranger. And teach them through your word to serve you and their fellowman through all the days of their lives. Through Jesus Christ our Lord and Savior. Amen.

Exchange of Vows

Minister: Richard, will you receive Debbie to be your wife, to build a home together under God, to give yourself fully in the sacred relationship of husband and wife? Will you freely give her your love? Will you respect her? Will you always be honest with her? Will you stand by her, comfort her, watch over her — either when she is sick or enjoying good health? And will you forsake all others and keep yourself only for her?

Groom: I will.

Minister: Debbie, will you now receive Richard to be your husband, to build a home together under God, to give yourself fully in the sacred relationship of husband and wife? Will you freely give him your love? Will you respect him? Will you always be honest with him? Will you stand by him, comfort him, watch over him — either when he is sick or enjoying good health? And will you forsake all others and keep yourself only for him?

Bride: I will.

Giving in Marriage

Minister: Who brings Debbie to present to Richard?

Parents of bride: We do.

Minister: Mr. and Mrs. Johnson and Mr. and Mrs. Morgan, are you willing to support and strengthen this marriage with your love and concern?

Parents: We are.

Further Exchange of Vows

Minister: Richard and Debbie, will you now hold hands and face each other. Richard, repeat this vow after me:

> I, Richard Morgan, receive you, Debbie Johnson,
> As a gift from God.
> I joyfully receive you to become my partner,
> To love and to cherish from this day forward —
> In times of sorrow and times of joy,
> In times of poverty and times of prosperity,
> In times of sickness and times of good health —
> To love and to enjoy
> Until death shall separate us.

Minister: Debbie, will you now repeat this vow after me. (The bride repeats the same vow as the groom.)

Exchange of Rings

Minister: When God made a covenant with Noah, he set a rainbow in the clouds and said, "I will look upon it that I may remember that it is an everlasting covenant." You have chosen rings as tokens of your marriage covenant. They are made of gold, a metal that is not easily tarnished and one that endures forever. These rings are an endless circle. They symbolize the unbroken marital union which is ordained and sanctioned by God. Let us ask God for his blessing as you prepare to exchange these rings.

Minister: Loving Father, we ask that you bless these rings as tokens of Richard's love for Debbie and of her love for him. May these rings become constant reminders of the promises they have made to each other this day. May their love forever encircle each other, as these rings encircle their fingers. Allow these rings, O Lord, to remind them also of your love that surrounds their hearts through Christ, who has brought us into the circle of your love. In his name we pray. Amen.

Groom (to the bride): I give you this ring. Wear it as a token of my love.

Bride: I accept your ring. I will wear it gladly as a token of your love. I also give you this ring. I hope you will wear it as a token of my love.

Groom: I accept your ring. I will wear it gladly as a token of your love.

Declaration of Marriage by the Minister

Richard and Debbie, we have rejoiced with you today as you have pledged your love and devotion to each other. Now, by the authority entrusted to me through Christ and in accordance with the laws of this state, I do hereby declare that you are husband and wife.

Lighting of Unity Candle plus
Gift of Roses to Parents

Minister (to the wedding guests): In just a moment Richard and Debbie will light one central candle from the two candles you see burning. This ceremony will symbolize the merging of their lives into one relationship. Following the candlelighting ceremony, they will each give their parents a rose. The roses symbolize the nurture provided by these parents since their children were very young. Richard and Debbie will give the roses as a symbol of their love and appreciation for their parents and all they have done for them.

Concluding Charge by the Minister

Richard and Debbie, be merciful, kind, and loving to each other. Accept life as a gift from God and your marriage as an opportunity for fulfillment. Be patient with one another. Forgive as freely as the Lord has forgiven you. And above everything else, be truly loving. Let the peace of Christ rule in your hearts and in your marriage, remembering that you have promised this day to live in harmony and love forever. And never forget to be thankful for what God has given you in each other.

Introduction of the Newlyweds

Minister: Ladies and gentlemen, I proudly introduce to you Mr. and Mrs. Richard Morgan.

A CEREMONY
WITH ACTIVE PARTICIPATION BY THE WEDDING PARTY
AND THE GUESTS

The following ceremony is a good example of a wedding where everyone gets in on the action — bride, groom, parents, even the guests. The bride and groom wrote their own vows and said them to each other without direction or guidance from the minister. The father of the bride didn't "give away" his daughter. Instead, he escorted her to the altar, then addressed the groom and his parents about the merger of two separate family traditions that was taking place that day. The wedding guests affirmed their blessing on the marriage by participating in a congregational response, led by the officiating minister.

If participation is what you want in your wedding ceremony, this service should give you some good ideas.

Opening Words of the Minister

Dear friends and loved ones of David and Joyce: Man has always felt compelled to celebrate the great moments of life. So he calls his friends and loved ones together to help commemorate these sacred occasions. Most of us want to share the great events of our lives with other people. But even more significantly, we feel the need to hold these joyful experiences up before God. Thus in this place of worship today, before their friends and loved ones and in the presence of God, David and Joyce come to speak their vows of marriage to each other. Will you please join with us as we praise the Lord for this happy occasion that brings us together.

Congregational Response

Minister: We have assembled here to worship with David and Joyce to share in the celebration of their marriage.

Congregation: As their friends and loved ones, we have come to help them celebrate this great moment in their lives. We rejoice that they have cultivated their love for each other. We affirm their desire and their right to join together in marriage.

Minister: David and Joyce have asked us to witness their covenant.

48

Congregation: As the witnessing community, we pledge our support to them as they begin their lives together. We pledge to open our community of fellowship to them while respecting their privacy as a new family unit.

Minister: We have come today to show our love for David and Joyce.

Congregation: As their friends and loved ones, we express our love for them. We will act as agents of God in giving them unconditional acceptance. We will support them in the joys and trials of their life together.

Prayer by the Minister and the Congregation

Minister: Now let us pause to ask God's blessing upon this union and upon our own lives as we pray the prayer our Lord taught us to pray, saying:

> Our Father which art in heaven,
> Hallowed be thy name,
> Thy kingdom come, they will be done,
> In earth as it is in heaven.
> Give us this day our daily bread
> And forgive us our trespasses
> As we forgive those who trespass against us.
> And lead us not into temptation
> But deliver us from evil —
> For thine is the kingdom, and the power,
> And the glory forever. Amen.

Giving in Marriage

Minister (speaking to the father of the bride): Mr. Campbell, you and Mrs. Campbell are to be commended for the fine job you have done in guiding Joyce to this point in her life. Are there any special words you would like to say on this happy occasion?

Father of the bride (to the minister): Yes, I would like to say a few words to the parents of the groom as well as to our future son-in-law on this occasion.

To the groom's parents: Mr. and Mrs. Turner, my wife and I are pleased to ask you to accept our daughter, Joyce, as your daughter, too. Thank you for the Christian values which you have taught your son. We have grown to love and respect David, and we are pleased today to receive him into our hearts as a son.

To the groom: David, we are pleased to present our daughter, Joyce, to be joined to you as wife during this ceremony. We have come to know you as a person of Christian integrity who is seeking to follow God's will. We proudly receive you today as a son. We commit Joyce to you in complete confidence that you will care for her needs and seek to make her happy in Christian love and marriage.

Exchange of Vows

Minister: Christian marriage is a total commitment of a man and a woman to each other for a lifetime. David and Joyce, will you now hold hands as you face each other and make your pledges of devotion and commitment.

Groom: Joyce, I believe that God brought us together and that he has led me to love you with a deep and abiding love. I promise that I will give you the kind of love that will help you reach your full potential as a person created in God's image. I will cherish you with tender love for the rest of our lives, even as Christ loved his bride, the church. I promise to work faithfully at cultivating our relationship so our love will grow stronger with each moment we share.

Bride: David, I return your love. I also believe that God brought us together and that he has led me to love you with a deep and abiding love. I will give you the kind of loving support that God intends a Christian wife to give her husband. I will cherish you with tender love and respect for the rest of our lives, even as the church honors Christ as her Lord. And I pray that our love for God and for one another will grow stronger with each day that we share together as husband and wife.

Exchange of Rings

Minister: The ring is a symbol of the love you have for each other. Its unending circle represents the eternal quality of your love. And the gold in these rings symbolizes the purity of your love. Now you may seal your promises to each other by giving and receiving the rings.

Groom: Joyce, I offer you this ring as a symbol of my enduring love. I ask that you wear it to show others that you are touched by my love.

Bride: I gladly accept your ring as a token of your love and I ask you also to accept my ring. I give it as a symbol of my love and devotion.

Declaration of Marriage

Minister: David and Joyce, heaven and earth and all the people assembled here have heard your mutual pledges of love and devotion to each other. Since you have promised to be true to each other for the rest of your lives, it is my distinct privilege now as a minister of the gospel to declare you husband and wife. May the grace of God go with you as you set about the task of building a Christian home.

Introduction of the Newlyweds

Minister: I present to you Mr. and Mrs. David Turner.

A CEREMONY
IN COMBINATION WITH A WORSHIP SERVICE

More and more couples seem to be taking the traditional church wedding one step further by scheduling their marriage during a regular hour of worship. This is especially appropriate if the couple happen to be active and faithful members of the church. What better way for the community of faith to show its concern for marriage and the family than to arrange a worship service around a Christian wedding?

The following ceremony occurred during the regular Sunday evening worship service of a church. Members of the church participated by singing traditional hymns of the faith. Members of the wedding party shared their faith by reading appropriate passages of Scripture at the beginning of the ceremony and leading prayers of intercession and thanksgiving at the end of the service. The minister presented a brief meditation on the meaning of love as portrayed in 1 Corinthians 13. After the ceremony, the wedding party participated in the celebration of the Lord's Supper with the rest of the congregation.

Invocation

Minister: Eternal God our Father, as you blessed the wedding at Cana in Galilee by the presence of your Son, so by his presence now make the occasion of this wedding one of rejoicing. Look with favor upon Barbara and Tony, about to be united in marriage. Grant that they, rejoicing in your gifts, may someday celebrate with Christ the Bridegroom the marriage feast which has no end.

Congregational Singing

Hymn: "Joyful, Joyful, We Adore Thee"

Scripture Reading

Maid of Honor: Genesis 2:18-24
Best Man: 1 Corinthians 12:31-13:13
Minister: John 2:1-10

Sermon

Minister: "These Abide: Faith, Hope, and Love" (1 Corinthians 13)

Congregational Singing

Hymn: "Be Thou My Vision"

Opening Words of the Minister

The Lord God in his goodness created mankind male and female. By the gift of marriage, he founded human community in a joy that begins now on the earth and is brought to perfection in the life to come. But because of our sin and rebellion, the joy of marriage can be marred and the gift of the family can become a burden. Our obedience to God's direction in our lives can assure us of joy and gladness in all our family relationships. Barbara and Tony, honor God in your lives and he will honor your home with his abiding presence. In this spirit of obedience, will you now pledge your love and devotion to each other as husband and wife.

Exchange of Vows

Groom: I take you, Barbara, to be my wife, and these things I promise you: I will be faithful to you and honest with you. I will respect, trust, help, and care for you. I will forgive you as we have been forgiven. I will work with you to come to a more perfect understanding of ourselves, the world, and God in the days ahead. I pledge my love and devotion to you through the best and worst of what is to come as long as we live.

Bride: Tony, I take you to be my husband from this time onward — to join with you and to share all that is to come, to give and to receive, to speak and to listen, to inspire and to respond, and in all circumstances of our life together to be loyal to you with my whole life and with all my being.

Exchange of Rings

Minister: Barbara and Tony, will you now exchange rings to seal your pledges of love and devotion to each other.
Bride: This ring is a sign of my love and faithfulness.
Groom: This ring is a sign of my love and faithfulness.

Declaration of Marriage

Minister (to the congregation): Barbara and Tony, by their promises before God and in the presence of this congregation, have taken each other as husband and wife. They have been joined by the love of God, and man must not divide them. Blessed be the Father, the Son, and the Holy Spirit now and forever.

Minister (to the couple): The Lord God, who created our first parents and established them in marriage, establish and sustain you, that you may find delight in each other and grow in love all the days of your life together.

Parents (as they lay their hands on the heads of their children, who kneel at the altar): May you dwell in God's presence forever. May you be preserved in true and constant love.

Prayer of Intercession and Thanksgiving

Bridesmaid: Lord, we praise you for the joy which your servants, Barbara and Tony, have found in each other. Thank you for the hope and trust with which they have established this new relationship. Give to us such a sense of your constant love that we may use all our strength in a life of praise to you whose work alone endures forever.

Groomsman: Eternal God, Father of love, pour down your grace upon Barbara and Tony that they may fulfill the vows they have made to each other today. Grant that they might reflect your steadfast love in their life-long faithfulness to each other. From your great store of strength give them gentleness and patience, affection and understanding, courage and joy toward each other that they might continue to grow in your love forever. Through Jesus Christ our Lord. Amen.

Celebration of the Lord's Supper

(The bride and groom and members of the wedding party participate in this celebration, along with the rest of the congregation.)

---

[1]This wedding ceremony is adapted from "Updating the Marriage Ceremony" by William L. Trimyer, an article in *Proclaim*, April-May-June, 1976. Copyright © 1976 by The Sunday School Board of the Southern Baptist Convention, Nashville, Tennessee. All rights reserved. Used by permission.

A CEREMONY WITH AFFIRMATION
BY PARENTS AND CONGREGATION

The following contemporary ceremony includes a verbal affirmation of the couple by their parents and the entire company of wedding guests. This is a good technique for getting everyone involved in the wedding service.

Opening Words of the Minister

We as a community of friends are gathered here in God's presence to witness the marriage of Byron and Linda and to ask God to bless them.

We are called to rejoice in their happiness, to help them when they have trouble, and to remember them in our prayers. Marriage, like our creation as men and women, owes its existence to God. It is his will and purpose that a husband and wife should love each other throughout their lives and give themselves fully to each other in undying love and commitment. As we approach this sacred hour when they shall be united, let us pause to ask God's blessing upon their union.

Prayer by the Minister

Eternal God, our Creator and Redeemer, as you gladdened the wedding at Cana in Galilee by the presence of your Son, so by your presence now, shower your joy upon this wedding. In favor look upon this couple and grant that they, rejoicing in all your gifts, may at length celebrate with Christ the Bridegroom, the marriage feast which has no end. Through Jesus Christ our Lord. Amen.

Charge to Couple by the Minister

Byron and Linda, let me remind you that marriage is a sacred and holy relationship. It will require the very best from both of you. But it is also life's most fulfilling relationship. As you give yourselves to each other, you will find your lives made happy and complete. Claim God's promise of blessing upon your union by seeking his will and direction in your relationship as husband and wife.

Now, as you look forward to pledging your love to each other, hear the Bible's description of genuine love:

Love is patient; love is kind and envies no one. Love is never boastful, nor conceited, nor rude; never selfish, not quick to take offense. Love keeps no score of wrongs; does not gloat over sins of others, but delights in the truth. There is nothing love cannot face; there is no limit to its faith, its hope, and its endurance.

In a word, there are three things that last forever: faith, hope, and love; but the greatest of them all is love (1 Cor. 13:4-7, 13, NEB).

Affirmation by Parents and Wedding Guests

Minister (addressing the parents of bride and groom): Do you as parents promise to pray for and support your children in this new relationship which they enter as husband and wife? If so, each say, "I will."

Parents (in unison): I will.

Minister (addressing the wedding guests): All of you who witness these vows, will you do everything in your power to support and uphold these two persons in their marriage? Then say, "We will."

Congregation (in unison): We will.

Exchange of Vows

Minister (addressing bride and groom): Byron and Linda, will you now repeat your marriage vows to each other?

Groom: I take you, Linda, to be my wife. I promise before God and these witnesses to be your faithful husband, to share with you in plenty and in want, in joy and in sorrow, in sickness and in health, to forgive and strengthen you and to join with you so that together we may serve God and others as long as we both shall live.

Bride: I take you, Byron, to be my husband. I promise before God and these witnesses to be your faithful wife, to share with you in plenty and in want, in joy and in sorrow, in sickness and in health, to forgive and strengthen you and to join with you so that together we may serve God and others as long as we both shall live.

Exchange of Rings

Minister (in a prayer of blessing for the rings): Bless, O Lord, these rings, that those who give them and wear them may do so in remembrance of their vows and covenant here made. May they abide in your will and continue in your favor throughout all their life, through Jesus Christ our Lord. Amen.

Groom (repeating after the minister): I give you this ring, as a symbol of my love and devotion, in the name of the Father, and of the Son, and of the Holy Spirit.

Bride (repeating after the minister): I give you this ring, as a symbol of my love and devotion, in the name of the Father, and of the Son, and of the Holy Spirit.

Declaration of Marriage by the Minister

Because Byron and Linda have made their vows with each other before God and all of us here, I declare them to be husband and wife in accordance with the will of God. Let no one divide those whom God has united.

Prayer of Thanksgiving by the Minister

O God, Creator and Father of us all, we thank you for the gift of marriage. We praise you for all the joys that come to us through marriage, and for the blessings of home and family.

Today, especially, we think of Byron and Linda as they begin their life together as husband and wife. Thank you for the joy they find in each other. Give them strength, Father, to keep the vows they have made. Help them to cherish the love they share, that they may be faithful and devoted to each other. Enrich their love with patience, understanding, wisdom, and honesty so they may establish a home dedicated to you and your will for their lives. Through Jesus Christ our Lord. Amen.

Lighting of the Unity Candle

Minister (as couple lights central candle with their individual candles): The Word of God declares, "For this cause shall a man leave his father and his mother, and cleave to his wife. And they two shall be one."

Benediction by the Minister

Minister (as couple kneels before him): Now may God the Father, God the Son, God the Holy Spirit, bless, preserve, and keep you; the Lord mercifully with his favor look upon you, and fill you with all spiritual benediction and grace; that you may faithfully live together in this life, and in the world to come have life everlasting. Through Jesus Christ our Lord. Amen.

A CEREMONY WITH RESPONSIVE VOWS
AND PRAYERS BY THE BRIDE AND GROOM

The following beautiful ceremony included vows written by the bride and groom and spoken to each other in responsive fashion. This wedding also featured brief but appropriate prayers voiced by the couple at the end of the wedding as well as participation by the wedding guests at several points in the service.

Prelude

"Praise to the Lord the Almighty"

56

Vocal Music

"Though I Speak with the Tongues"

Processional

"Praise Ye the Father"

Opening Words of the Minister

Dear friends, we are assembled here today in the presence of God to unite Don and Kathryn in marriage. The Bible teaches that marriage should be a permanent relationship of one man and one woman freely and totally committed to each other for a lifetime. Jesus himself declared that man shall leave his father and mother and woman shall leave her home to be united with each other in a pledge of total commitment.

Marriage that lasts must be built on the secure foundation of love. In the thirteenth chapter of First Corinthians, the Apostle Paul gives a beautiful description of the type of love it takes to build a happy home:

> Love is patient; love is kind and envies no one. Love is never boastful, nor conceited, nor rude; never selfish, not quick to take offense. Love keeps no score of wrongs; does not gloat over other men's sins, but delights in the truth. There is nothing love cannot face; there is no limit to its faith, its hope, and its endurance (1 Cor. 13:4-7, 13, NEB).

Love like this can bring honor to God in our homes. Don and Kathryn, my fervent prayer is that your marriage will always be blessed with an abundance of this kind of love.

Would you as the congregation please join me in reading responsively from the wedding bulletin to pledge your support to Don and Kathryn as they take this important step in their lives.

Responsive Reading by Wedding Guests

MINISTER: Don and Kathryn covet our prayers and support as they begin the pilgrimage of marriage together.

CONGREGATION: We promise to uphold them in our thoughts and prayers as they work at building a deep and everlasting love.

MINISTER: We must remind ourselves that genuine love is not easily achieved. Don and Kathryn will need determination and patience to renew their

57

	vows year after year. Genuine love is not static; it must be constantly renewed.
CONGREGATION:	We promise to support them in every appropriate way as they work at this task in their marriage.
MINISTER:	We also realize that genuine love is fulfilled only as it reaches out to others. We ask that the unique love which Don and Kathryn feel for each other might reach out beyond themselves to their family, their friends, and the larger world in which they live.
CONGREGATION:	We promise to return this love as it flows out to us. And we, in turn, will pass this love on to the larger universe in which we dwell. This is God's purpose in giving us the gift of love — that is might expand and grow to bless the lives of others.

Preparation for Exchange of Vows

Minister: Don and Kathryn, you have heard this expression of support from your family and friends. Are you now prepared to seal your sacred union as husband and wife?

Bride and Groom: We are.

Minister: Then join hands and express your marriage vows to each other.

Exchange of Vows

Groom: Kathryn, I want to state it clearly so all the people here will understand: I love you and I want you to become my wife.

Bride: Don, I gladly accept the privilege of becoming your wife. I also declare openly and honestly that I love you and I want you to become my husband.

Groom: I promise to put you first in my life. I will always try to remember that our love for each other is our most important possession.

Bride: I also pledge to hold you first in my heart. I promise to work at building a strong, secure relationship that will stand the test of time and the ups and downs of life.

Groom: I will be faithful to you always.

Bride: And I will be faithful to you.

Unison: Whatever the future holds, we will face it together. We make these promises gladly in a spirit of joyful love.

Congregational Hymn

"Pass It On"

Exchange of Rings

Minister: The perfect circle of a ring symbolizes eternity, while gold is a symbol of all that is pure and holy. As you give these rings to each other, our prayer is that your love for each other will be as eternal and everlasting as these beautiful rings.

Groom (as he places the ring on bride's finger): Kathryn, with this ring I symbolize our union as husband and wife—for today, tomorrow, and all the years to come. Please wear it as a reminder of our deep and abiding love.

Bride (as she places the ring on groom's finger): Don, I also give you this ring as a symbol of our union as husband and wife—for today, tomorrow, and all the years to come. Please wear it as a reminder of our deep and abiding love.

Affirmation of Congregation

Minister: All of you who have witnessed these vows (turning to the congregation), will you do everything in your power to support and uphold Don and Kathryn in their marriage? Then say, "We will."

Congregation: We will.

Declaration of Marriage and Charge by the Minister

Don and Kathryn, since you have made your marriage vows with each other and before all of us assembled here, I now pronounce that you are husband and wife, in accordance with God's holy purpose. Let me remind you to be merciful, kind, and forgiving toward each other. Accept life as a good gift from God and your marriage as an opportunity for highest fulfillment. Forgive each other as freely as God has forgiven you. And above all, be truly loving, growing in the knowledge and grace of the Lord Jesus Christ. Now you may light the unity candle to symbolize your union as husband and wife.

Lighting of the Unity Candle

Minister: (as bride and groom light the central candle with their individual candles): The Bible declares that the man shall leave his home and the woman shall leave her family and they shall become as one in a new relationship. In this mystic union they share a togetherness that gives them strength for all the circumstances of our earthly pilgrimage.

Congregation (in unison): As it was in the beginning, it is now until the end.

Prayer of Thanks by Bride and Groom

Minister: Don and Kathryn, in this sacred hour, each of you may voice a prayer of thanks for the joys and privileges you now face as husband and wife.

Groom: Lord, thank you for the joy I feel on this special day. Thank you for bringing us together as husband and wife. Make me a thoughtful and considerate husband, and go with us as we face the challenge of building a Christian home. In Jesus' name.

Bride: Dear Father, thank you for your abiding presence on this our wedding day. Thank you for our families and friends whose love and support we have also felt. Continue to guide and direct us as we face the future together as a married couple. In Jesus' name we pray. Amen.

Concluding Prayer of the Minister

Eternal God our Father, go now with Don and Kathryn on their journey into marriage. Impress the memories of this day upon their minds so they can draw strength and inspiration from this occasion in the days ahead. Fill them with such love and joy that they may build a loving, accepting, and forgiving home, in accordance with your will.

Now the Lord bless you and keep you; the Lord make his face to shine upon you, and be gracious unto you; the Lord lift up his countenance upon you and give you peace, both now and forevermore. Through Jesus Christ our Lord. Amen.

Presentation of the Couple by the Minister

It is my privilege to present to you Mr. and Mrs. Don Prentice.

Recessional

"Now Thank We All Our God"

NOTES

NOTES

_____

_____

_____

_____

_____

_____

_____

_____

_____

_____

_____

_____

_____

_____

_____

_____

_____

_____

5

Tips for Planning
Your Own Ceremony

Now that you have studied all the ideas in this book, you are ready to start planning your own unique wedding service. Here are some planning tips to help you get your ceremony firmed up and ready before the big day arrives.

PLAN TOGETHER
AS BRIDE AND GROOM

Don't make the mistake of planning what you want in a wedding service, then presenting it to your fiancé for his or her approval. Gone are the days when the bride made all the key decisions about the wedding. Most young couples today want their wedding to be a joint effort — a unique expression of their relationship. Planning your ceremony together will take more time, but at least you'll be assured that both of you are committed to it when the final product rolls off the assembly line!

Another plus of planning together is that you'll probably get some new insights into your fiancé's values and personality traits — some good, some not so good. Isn't this better than making those shocking discoveries a month or two after the wedding is over?

START EARLY

Start planning your ceremony several months before the wedding date. This will give you time to think thoroughly about every ingredient of your service — maybe even to change your mind several times, if necessary. Remember, the ceremony is only one of dozens of details you'll have to plan. So don't box yourself in by waiting until the final month before the wedding to think about the type of service you want.

CONSULT WITH THE MINISTER

Before you go too far with your planning, consult with the officiating minister. Make sure he is open to the idea of using a ceremony of your creation in the wedding. He may have a standard ceremony that he prefers to use in all the weddings he conducts. If so, let him know that you and your fiancé plan to do all the work of writing the ceremony. Assure him that he can check the ceremony after you've completed it to make sure it is thoroughly Christian.

Most ministers don't object to the bride and groom writing their own ceremony, as long as they are consulted early in the planning process. This is a courtesy that you should show to your minister as soon as you decide you want something a little different in your ceremony. And besides, he might have some additional resources and some great ideas from other weddings that you can use in creating your own service.

OBSERVE OTHER WEDDINGS

Speaking of ideas, other weddings are some of the best idea sources available. Ask all your friends who have had weddings recently to share copies of their ceremonies. Try to attend several weddings with your fiancé to observe the "flow" of a typical ceremony and to isolate some specific features that appeal to both of you. This "field experience" can supplement your theoretical planning and help you focus on ceremony features that hold up under the test of a real, live wedding.

BALANCE THE CONTEMPORARY WITH THE TRADITIONAL

One good rule to remember as you plan your ceremony is the principle of balance. Try to balance every new and innovative feature with some traditional element that will be instantly recognized by your wedding guests. Otherwise, you may end up with a ceremony so modern and radical that it comes across as cold and unfeeling. Remember that human beings find comfort and security in the familiar. Your object should be to strike a happy balance between the old and the new as you plan the service.

PUT THE CEREMONY IN WRITING

After you and your fiancé have agreed on all the elements you want to include in your ceremony, consult with the minister again to make sure it meets with his approval. After his O.K., you are ready to put the ceremony in writing.

In this final draft of your wedding service, include thorough instructions on every detail — where members of the wedding party stand, what the minister says at every point in the ceremony, when the wedding party leaves the church, etc. Writing down every detail like this won't guarantee a flawless ceremony, but it certainly beats leaving everything to chance.

CONSIDER PUBLISHING
A WEDDING BULLETIN

After you have worked out all the details of your ceremony and the rest of the wedding, think about printing a wedding bulletin to distribute to your wedding guests. This bulletin should include information about all the essential features of your wedding — date, place, names of members of the wedding party, details about the reception, and an outline of the ceremony. Some couples even include every word spoken during the ceremony. A detailed bulletin like this would contain vows to each other, pronouncements of the minister, and other statements by members of the wedding party. It's strictly up to you how detailed or how general you want your wedding bulletin to be. But some printed memento of your wedding, no matter how sketchy, is definitely a good idea. In the years ahead you'll treasure a copy of your wedding bulletin because it serves as a visible, historical reminder of one of the most important days in your life.

For a good example of what to aim for in your wedding bulletin, turn to the sample wedding bulletin on pages 83-86 of this book. This folder was hand-lettered by the mother of the bride, then reproduced by a local printer for distribution to the wedding guests. It has a stylish, contemporary look, but it also comes across as warm and personal. These are the elements you should strive for as you plan your wedding bulletin. It should complement the unique, personal ceremony that you and your fiance have created especially for this big event.

MAKE NEEDED CHANGES
DURING THE REHEARSAL

Your ceremony probably won't get its first true "trial run" until the rehearsal a day or two before the wedding. Chances are a few minor changes will be necessary to make your ceremony "flow" a little smoother. So try to hang loose and watch for places where the ceremony could be improved with a few minor adjustments. When you're creating your own ceremony, it's impossible to foresee every little complication that might arise when the wedding is being staged for real. But a cooperative spirit and a willingness to compromise on certain details will take care of most of these problems.

By now you're probably convinced that writing your own wedding ceremony requires a lot of hard work. You're right; it does. But it can also be a fun experience with many lasting rewards. Thousands of couples before you have created their own ceremonies. And most of them would do it again if they were in your shoes.

So what are you waiting for? On with the task!

NOTES

_____

_____

_____

_____

_____

_____

_____

_____

_____

_____

_____

_____

NOTES

NOTES

_____

_____

_____

_____

_____

_____

_____

_____

_____

_____

_____

_____

_____

_____

_____

_____

_____

6
Put It in Writing:
Your Own Ceremony in
Outline Form

You noticed in Chapter 5 that the final step in planning your own unique wedding ceremony is to put it in writing. The rehearsal for your wedding and the actual service will go much smoother if you have a fully-detailed outline of all the main ingredients of that special event. This section of the book is designed to help you as you begin to pull together a general outline of your own ceremony.

First, you and your fiancé should read this *Idea Book* thoroughly. Then begin to discuss some of the suggestions from the book that you would like to include in your wedding. Write down these ideas in the appropriate spaces on the following pages. Add other ideas that you pick up from other weddings in the weeks and months ahead. With further polish and adaptation as you plan together, this rough outline should begin to shape up into a finished ceremony, with every detail spelled out, before the big day arrives.

MUSIC FOR THE WEDDING

Prelude: _____

_____

_____

_____

Processional: _____

_____

_____

_____

Vocal Music: _____

_____

_____

_____

Recessional: _____

_____

_____

_____

WORDS OF WELCOME FROM THE COUPLE

_____

_____

_____

_____

_____

_____

_____

_____

_____

_____

_____

_____

_____

_____

_____

OPENING WORDS OF THE MINISTER

PRAYERS OF THE MINISTER
AND MEMBERS OF THE WEDDING PARTY

_____

_____

_____

_____

_____

_____

_____

_____

_____

_____

_____

_____

_____

_____

SCRIPTURE PASSAGES

_____

_____

_____

_____

_____

_____

_____

_____

_____

_____

_____

_____

_____

_____

POETRY

_____

_____

_____

_____

_____

_____

_____

_____

_____

_____

_____

_____

_____

_____

_____

THE GIVING IN MARRIAGE

_____

_____

_____

_____

_____

_____

_____

_____

_____

_____

_____

_____

_____

_____

CONGREGATIONAL RESPONSES

_____

_____

_____

_____

_____

_____

_____

_____

_____

_____

_____

_____

_____

_____

_____

_____

_____

_____

EXCHANGE OF VOWS

EXCHANGE OF RINGS

_____

_____

_____

_____

_____

_____

_____

_____

_____

_____

_____

_____

_____

_____

_____

_____

LIGHTING OF THE UNITY CANDLE

_____

_____

_____

_____

_____

_____

_____

_____

_____

_____

_____

_____

_____

_____

DECLARATION OF MARRIAGE
BY THE MINISTER

_____

_____

_____

_____

_____

_____

_____

_____

_____

_____

_____

_____

_____

_____

_____

_____

NOTES

A Ceremony
Celebrating the Marriage
of
Jennifer Ann Ray
and
Mark Stefan Klein

Saturday, September 12, 1981
at two in the afternoon
First Baptist Church
Nashville, Tennessee

The Ceremony

Lighting of the Candles   Greg Klein
                          Daniel Ray

Organ Prelude   Richard Brown

   The King of Love My Shepherd Is   Milford

   Aria in F Major   Handel

   Let Us Ever Walk with Jesus   Buszin

   If Thou But Suffer God to Guide Thee - Johnson

   Joyful, Joyful We Adore Thee   Hymn to Joy

   O Perfect Love   Dustin

   If Thou Art Near   Bach

   Saviour Like a Shepherd Lead Us   Bock

Solo — Because   D'Hardelet
           David Ford

Seating of the Mothers

Solo — Prayer of St. Francis Assisi   Dungan
           David Ford

Processional
      Trumpet Voluntary   Jeremiah Clark

Comments on Christian Marriage
          H. Franklin Paschall

Giving of the Bride by her Father

Solo — How Do I Love Thee   Lippe
          David Ford

Reflections on Christian Love
             Rayburn W. Ray

Exchanging of the Vows

Benediction
   Solo — The Lord's Prayer   Malotte
          David Ford

Presentation of the New Family

Recessional — Wedding March — Mendelssohn

Doxology   Bock

Reception following in the church parlor.

Assisting at the Reception

Melanie Gray	Catherine Relfe
Barbara Klein	Floris Relfe
Sara Miller	Joan Rollins
Jean Olson	Augusta Salem

Tara Seeley

The Wedding Party

Ministers	H. Franklin Paschall
	Rayburn W. Ray
Soloist	David Ford
Musicians	Organ – Richard Brown
	Piano – Linda Ford

Matron of Honor – Linda Dufresne, Chicago

Maid of Honor – Nora Frances Stone, Jackson, Ms.

Bridesmaids

Laura Barker	Birmingham
Cindy Boatwright	New York
Debbie Mader	Birmingham
Sallie Roper	Durham, N.C.

Best Man – Rock Klein Washington, D.C.

Groomsmen

Lauren Harsted	Phoenix
Dan Kendree	Phoenix
Greg Klein	Chicago
David Luhr	Los Angeles
Daniel Ray	Nashville

Calligraphy by Rose Ann Ray, the bride's mother.

NOTES

Countdown to a Perfect Wedding

In addition to creating your own ceremony, there are scores of other details you must take care of in advance to make sure your wedding goes smoothly. Some of these important events are listed here. As you complete each item, check it off and write the completion date in the appropriate space.

4-6 MONTHS BEFORE THE WEDDING

DATE COMPLETED

_____ Consult with minister; set wedding date . . . . _____

_____ Reserve church; review all policies concerning weddings in church building . . . . _____

_____ Reserve meeting place for reception; select a caterer . . . . _____

_____ Begin compiling a guest list . . . . _____

_____ Select a florist; make arrangements for flowers . . . . _____

_____ Select attendants . . . . _____

_____ Arrange for music; consult with organist, soloist . . _____

_____ Order invitations and thank you cards . . . . _____

_____ Agree with fiancé on who will pay for various services; communicate these agreements to parents of the bride and groom . . . . _____

2-3 MONTHS BEFORE THE WEDDING

_____ Plan wedding ceremony, in consultation with minister . . . . _____

_____ Start addressing invitations . . . . _____

_____ Make reservations for wedding trip . . . . _____

_____ Select wedding rings and have them engraved . . . . . _____

_____ Order wedding dress and attendants' dresses; reserve formal wear for wedding party . . . . _____

_____ Make arrangements for wedding photographs . . . . _____

_____ Mail wedding announcement to local newspaper . . _____

_____ Enlist people to assist at reception . . . . _____

_____ Select a person to keep the guest book . . . . _____

_____ Select a person to receive gifts at church on
wedding day . . . . _____

1 MONTH BEFORE THE WEDDING

_____ Mail invitations . . . . _____

_____ Start writing thank you notes as gifts arrive . . . . . . _____

_____ Buy gifts for attendants . . . . _____

Plan food and accommodations for out-of-town
guests. . . . . _____

_____ Prepare follow-up article about wedding for local
newspaper. . . . . _____

_____ Complete all arrangements for rehearsal and
rehearsal dinner . . . . _____

_____ Secure marriage license . . . . _____

2 WEEKS BEFORE THE WEDDING

_____ Have the wedding bulletins printed . . . . _____

_____ Double-check all details about the rehearsal and the
ceremony with the minister . . . . _____

_____ Double-check all reservations and details with
florist, caterer, photographer, musicians, formal
wear agency, etc. . . . . _____

Make arrangements for someone to tape-record
ceremony; check to see that church lighting and
sound systems are working . . . . _____

Tape?

ON THE WEDDING DAY

_____ Arrange to take several cars to the church to
transport clothing, gifts, guests, wedding party,
etc. . . . . _____

_____ Make sure church is unlocked early for wedding
party; arrange for entry to dressing rooms,
sanctuary, organ, etc. . . . . _____

_____ Take needle and thread, extra pins, etc., for
last-minute fitting emergencies . . . . _____

_____ Have fees ready to pay minister, organist,
custodian, etc. . . . . _____

AFTER THE WEDDING

_____ Now that it's all over, relax and enjoy your
wedding trip! . . . . _____

_____ Finish writing and mailing thank you notes . . . . _____

NOTES

NOTES

NOTES

NOTES

NOTES

NOTES

NOTES